JUICES AND
SMOOTHIES

MORE THAN 80 ENERGISING IDEAS

JUICES AND SMOOTHIES

MORE THAN 80 ENERGISING IDEAS

MURDOCH BOOKS

contents

squeeze it When life has run you ragged, and even when it hasn't, there is a place close by where help can be found. Let the kitchen be more than just a nod to necessary sustenance — make it shine with some mighty fine juice concoctions. All you need are some fresh fruit and vegetables, a juicer or blender and a little inspiration, and you'll soon have a whole lot of healing going on.

squeeze it

Many people make fresh juices at home as a way to look after their health. And with very good reason — a glass of fresh fruit or vegetable juice is an excellent way to get a little nutrition into one's system. Fresh juices can repair, protect, energize and improve — not just the body, but the mind and spirit as well. These are serious benefits. However, other people make their own juices because they taste good. This is also very valid: juices are delicious. As well, they are convenient, cheap and easy to make. Anyone can make them, without needing fancy equipment or culinary skills.

But more than health ... more than nutritional balance ... more than even the time-saving benefits of a cleansing breakfast in a glass ... the reason people *really* squeeze, juice and blend every day across the nation is because we're all budding scientists and artists at heart. Juicing allows you to bring your own creative interpretation to nature's bounty, to bring some order to the chaos of the fruit bowl and a little sense to the vegetables. Juicing lets us take A + B and make C. What's more, there's lots of noise, and things splash about, and different sizes and shapes go in, and liquid comes out, and it may be slushy or smooth or frothy and thick, and is sometimes sunset pink, but other times deep crimson or vivid green — and we're the ones controlling the whole thing. Miraculous!

There are few times in life when you can give free rein to your inner kitchen artist, and feel safe in the knowledge that the results will rarely be less than excellent or beneficial. What could be better?

the good juice

The health benefits associated with regularly drinking fresh fruit and vegetable juices are many and of long standing. We're not talking about some new-fangled fad here. But, equally, there's no time better than the present to repeat them. Juices provide energy to the energy-deficient, protect the immune system, have cleansing and settling properties, give encouragement to a flagging libido, and even make it a bit easier to get going in the morning. Fresh fruit and vegetables contain an amazing array of vitamins, minerals and other trace elements that are known to be essential for good health, and digesting them in liquid form is one of the best ways to help them on their beneficial way. No commercially-prepared juice is going to have the same fresh goodness as your own drink will. The following is a taste of the good things juices contain:

antioxidants are powerful protective substances that neutralize potentially harmful molecules found in the body. These molecules, known as free radicals, are normal by-products of metabolism, but factors such as stress, smoking and pollution can boost their numbers. If left unchecked, free radicals may play a role in the onset of heart disease, osteoporosis and cancer. Some key antioxidants are vitamin E (wheat germ, spinach, avocado), vitamin C (citrus and tropical fruits, green vegetables, berries); and beta-carotene (apricots, dark leafy greens, mangoes, tomatoes, watercress).

The body can't make minerals but it sure does need them. They are present in the body in small amounts, and are essential for numerous jobs ranging from regulating blood pressure to keeping teeth strong and healthy. All of the seven major minerals and nine of the various trace elements are vital to good health. Found in rich supply in fresh juices are minerals such as calcium (dairy, figs and fortified soy products); iron (dried apricots, green leafy vegetables, spinach, nuts); magnesium (nuts, especially almonds); potassium (bananas, dried fruits, tea) and zinc (eggs).

phytochemicals are compounds found naturally in plants. They do not have a nutritional

value but are thought to be needed by the body for disease prevention. 'Thought to be' because they're secretive little critters, but ongoing research suggests that phytochemicals can lower the risk of osteoporosis, cancer and inflammatory disorders. The only way to guarantee you get enough phytochemicals is by eating and drinking a wide variety of different coloured fruit and vegetables of the best possible quality.

You may well ask what vitamins aren't needed for: they are vital to fundamental processes such as growth, reproduction and tissue repair; are essential for the normal functioning of every organ in the body; and are also needed to release the energy from dietary carbohydrate, fat, protein and alcohol. Like minerals, most vitamins cannot be made in the body, so must be supplied by the diet. The following vitamins are found in good amounts in fruit and vegetables: the B vitamins (bananas, dried fruits, soy products, wheat germ); vitamin C (citrus fruits, green vegetables, berries, tomatoes, some tropical fruit); and vitamin E (wheat germ, spinach, avocado, nuts).

Who would have thought that fruit and vegetables were so well equipped to fight the good fight? But they are, and so much the better for us.

the juice on juicers

Most juices and smoothies are made with one of two pieces of equipment — a juicer or a blender. Some recipes require both; others also involve the use of a citrus press. But that's about it.

There is no question that the best juicers are expensive and, for most of us, the hardest part about making fresh juices at home is the initial decision to buy the thing. That, and working out where to put it. When choosing a juicer, prices and reliability pretty much go hand in hand upwards, but here are a few things to consider before you buy: does the juicer have parts that are dishwasher proof; what is the motor's size; how easy will it be to clean; how wide is the chute (will it be able to cope with whole fruit and vegetables); does it have low and high speeds; and is there a slide-in froth separator (which is about as good as it gets)? The more expensive juicers generally do work better, and last longer. They also extract more juice per fruit so you get more for your money. Juicers work by a process of centrifugal motion, spinning the fruit or vegetable pieces in a filter basket fitted with a rotating cutting disk, thus separating the juice from the pulp. The juice comes out the spout; the leftover pulp goes into its own disposal container. A few things to remember: always use the plunger to push food down the chute, not your fingers; use the plunger slowly (this will ensure the greatest amount of juice is extracted from the pulp, and will ease the strain on the filter basket and motor); and put the juice jug or a glass under the spout before turning on. If you wish, line the pulp-collecting container with a plastic bag, as that can be easily discarded later. Do not let the pulp-collecting container overfill. Fruit and vegetables with a high water content, like tomatoes and watermelon, should be juiced on the slower speed (if your machine has this option); and hard ingredients such as carrots, apples, beetroot and fennel work best on a higher speed. All juicers need cleaning. Sad but true. A few tips: always ensure the stainless steel filter is thoroughly clean before use. This means cleaning it properly immediately *after* each use. Once pulp dries on the filter, it will clog the pores and is a bore to remove. Watch fingers when cleaning the filter basket. Some juicers come with a special brush for washing the basket — use it. It will help.

As their name suggests, blenders mix and whizz ingredients to a smooth consistency. Look for ones that can cope with crushed ice cubes. Capacity

varies but the best are the stand alone ones, as they produce smoother drinks. But, really, any blender will do. Chop ingredients such as orchard fruits and bananas finely for best results. Blending ingredients such as plums will give drinks flecked with the skin.

The citrus press is an old stalwart. Be it a simple plastic job, a wooden reamer or a top-of-the-range chrome citrus press with handle, the process is pretty much the same. Take citrus, cut in half, place against citrus press, squeeze and twist. Strain the juice of pips if you wish, before drinking or combining with another juice. Always reliable, a citrus press is time efficient and easy to clean. If you don't have a citrus press, however, just peel the fruit (leaving as much white pith as possible), chop into chunks and pass through a juicer or blender.

getting a grip

There is not much that can go really wrong when squeezing, blending and whizzing your own fresh juices. But there are a few ways to guarantee great drinks every time. Always use good-quality ingredients — there is nothing to mask their flavours, after all. Use organic where possible, and refrain from using ingredients until they are fully ripe. Use fruit and vegetables straight from the refrigerator, so that the end result is perfectly chilled. If you freeze fruit, such as berries, cherries, chopped mango and overripe banana, use the fruit within two weeks. After that, the flavour fades. Unless otherwise stated, juice fruit and vegetables with the skin on. Remove all pits and hard stones before using. The seeds can stay if juicing but remove if blending. Wash produce before use, scrubbing tough-skinned varieties with a soft brush. Chop ingredients only when you are ready to chuck the pieces in the juicer or blender; otherwise you will cause unnecessary vitamin loss. Don't be shy — experiment, embellish, revise or adapt recipes to find your preferred flavour combinations. It's part of the pleasure. Adjust the consistency of drinks by adding water or still mineral water for a thinner drink, or frozen fruit, crushed ice or frozen yoghurt for a thicker one. Sweeten juices by adding a dash of honey, maple syrup or some ripe banana (though this will affect the drink's consistency). If adding sugar, always use caster (superfine) sugar as it dissolves easily. Experimentation will reveal if you like drinks rich and heavy, with ingredients such as bananas, or clean and sharp, with flavours like citrus and ginger. On the whole, fruit and veg don't mix. Of course, now that you've read that, the first recipe you see will be a **fruit and veg combo**. Give it a go. When juicing fresh herbs or small quantities of ingredients such as a piece of ginger or alfalfa sprouts bunch them together or send them through the juicer alternating with a main ingredient. Whole ice cubes can be added to the blender, but crushing them first gives a better result. There is also **something therapeutic** about smashing tea-towel-wrapped ice cubes against the kitchen bench or hitting them with a rolling pin. It's all part of the fun. Finally, drink juices immediately. If you wait, things start separating, colours change, nutritional value fades and the flavour goes all wrong. This is especially true of juices containing apple and pear, which oxidize quickly. There is no time like the present with fresh juices ...

berries'n'cherries Berries (and cherries and grapes), what words can describe thee? Bold, bright, bounteous (for some of the year), brazen yet blessed, beautiful, beneficial, bodacious and so berry berry beloved. (Little bundles of bursting brilliancy.) Such are these small, juicy fruit, appearing in their best purples and reds every spring and summer. Behold the berry! (And cherries and grapes.) Get into them.

Plump blackberries have a sweet, juicy flavour all their own. They are best used within 2 days of purchasing, or frozen for later use. blackcurrants bring a tartness to drinks that isn't suggested by their size. They are generally used in juice form, often mixed with other fruit juices. Sweet blueberries appear in late spring and are also available frozen. Little powerhouses, they are a fantastic source of antioxidants. Choose firm, plump berries and use within 1 week of buying. cherries need pitting before use. Use a cherry pitter or cut in half and remove the pit with your fingers. It's not that hard. Use fresh cherries within 1 week of buying, otherwise buy frozen, pitted cherries. Fresh cranberries are rare creatures — use dried cranberries or cranberry juice instead. Potassium-rich, naturally sweet grapes are excellent for balancing other stronger flavours. They ripen quickly at room temperature so are best stored in the refrigerator. Wash well to remove any insecticide. Buy fully ripe raspberries on the day they are to be eaten and avoid washing them, or wash them just before using, and handle them as little as possible. What raspberries lack in juice they more than offer in intense colour and flavour. Sieve the juice after blending, if liked. Freeze when in season and buy frozen, unsweetened ones when not. Choose strawberries that are plump, glossy, unbruised and firm and store in the refrigerator for up to 3 days. Wash and hull just before using. Use in the juicer or blender.

It's sweet, it's rich and it's full of what you need.

What's not to fall for?

blueberry crush

150 g (5¹/2 oz) blueberries
750 ml (3 cups) apple and blackcurrant juice
500 ml (2 cups) soda water
1 tablespoon caster (superfine) sugar
ice cubes, to serve

Blend the blueberries, apple and blackcurrant juice, soda water and sugar in a blender until smooth. Serve over ice. Makes 4 medium glasses.

Note: To make a slushy, add the ice cubes, crushed, to the blender when mixing the other ingredients.

Guaranteed not to leave you standing alone.

blue moon

300 g (10½ oz) blueberries
6 small peaches, stones removed
2 cm (¾ inch) piece ginger
pinch ground cinnamon
honey, to taste, optional
ice cubes, to serve

Juice the blueberries, peaches and ginger through a juice extractor. Stir through the cinnamon and honey, if desired, and serve over ice. Makes 2 small glasses.

Complex and sophisticated, the sweet fruit is mellowed by the deep bass notes of cold black tea.

cherry and berry punch

400 g (14 oz) cherries, pitted
200 g (7 oz) blackberries
200 g (7 oz) blueberries
125 g (4 1/2 oz) strawberries, hulled and halved
750 ml (3 cups) dry ginger ale
500 ml (2 cups) lemonade
250 ml (1 cup) cold black tea
zest of 1 lemon, cut into long thin strips
10 mint leaves, torn
ice cubes, to serve

Put the cherries, blackberries, blueberries, strawberries, dry ginger ale, lemonade, tea, lemon zest and mint into a jug. Cover the jug and chill for at least 3 hours. Add ice cubes to serve. Makes 10 small glasses.

Serve with sushi on a Friday night and say sayonara baby to the working week.

cherry blossom slushy

3 large Nashi pears, stalks removed
300 g (10^1/$_2$ oz) frozen pitted cherries
8–10 ice cubes, crushed

Juice the Nashi through a juice extractor. Add the Nashi juice, frozen cherries and ice cubes to a blender and process until smooth. Makes 2 medium glasses.

cherry blossom slushy

Apple, berry, cherry … let's start at the very beginning, the very best place to start! It's an elementary choice, really.

abc

150 g (5½ oz) raspberries
400 g (14 oz) cherries, pitted
6 apples, stalks removed
ice cubes, to serve

Juice the raspberries, cherries and apples through a juice extractor. Stir to combine and serve over ice. Makes 2 large glasses.

This pink tonic is just the ticket for a lazy afternoon game of tennis with the chaps.

raspberry lemonade

300 g (10½ oz) raspberries
275 g (1¼ cups) sugar
500 ml (2 cups) lemon juice
ice cubes, to serve
mint leaves, to garnish

Blend the raspberries and sugar in a blender until smooth. Push the mixture through a strong sieve and discard the seeds. Add the lemon juice, mix well and pour into a large jug. Stir through 1.5 litres (6 cups) water and chill well. Serve over ice, garnished with mint leaves. Makes 6 medium glasses.

This bird won't give you wings but it will help ground your immune system.

strange bird

500 g (1 lb 2 oz) strawberries, hulled
6 kiwifruit, peeled
ice cubes, to serve

Juice the strawberries and kiwifruit through a juice extractor. Stir to combine and serve over ice. Makes 2 small glasses.

Ramp up the passion factor with a zinger of a juice — serve just before bed!

strawberry, rockmelon and passionfruit juice

500 g (1 lb 2 oz) strawberries, hulled
1 small rockmelon (or other orange-fleshed melon), peeled,
   seeded and chopped
2 large passionfruit

Juice the strawberries and rockmelon through a juice extractor. Stir through the passionfruit pulp. Makes 2 medium glasses.

strange bird

Let the season guide your footsteps — choose whatever fresh berries are available.

mixed berry and lemonade fizz

100 g (3 1/2 oz) strawberries, hulled
50 g (1 3/4 oz) blueberries
750 ml (3 cups) lemonade
2 scoops lemon sorbet

Blend the strawberries, blueberries, lemonade and lemon sorbet in a blender until well combined. Pour into glasses and add any extra berries, if desired. Makes 4 small glasses.

A creamy cloud of fruity heaven, perfect for drifting along on a sunny afternoon.

strawberry, kiwi and peach slushy

250 g (9 oz) strawberries, hulled
2 kiwifruit, peeled and chopped
200 g (7 oz) canned peaches in natural juice
3 scoops orange sorbet or gelato

Blend the strawberries, kiwifruit, undrained peaches and sorbet or gelato in a blender until smooth. Makes 2 large glasses.

mixed berry and lemonade fizz

orchard fruits When apricots first came along, all things round, soft and bottom-like sat up and took notice. When peaches came along, blossoms and downy creatures took heart, while pears gave shape to artist's dreams, apples helped pies find their form and plums plumbed new depths. When things look glum, turn to orchard fruit. It's hard to remain down when faced with a soft, round, furry, yummy thing.

apples are ideally suited to juicing and blending: they need only washing, their stalk removed, and then cut into rough chunks before tossing into the chosen machine. They leave little mess when used in a juicer, and give a clear, cleansing drink. Avoid floury apples. Canned apples are good for blending. Velvety, ripe apricots are best used on the day of purchase. Remove the stones before juicing or blending. Canned apricots in natural juice and apricot nectar are both ideal for blending; dried apricots are suitable for infusions. Smooth-skinned nectarines are great in the juicer or blender. No need to peel but do remove the stone. The skin may fleck blended drinks. The same goes for peaches; juice or blend these babies. The height of summer is the time to indulge in peaches — this is when their flavour is at their fragrant, juicy best. Again, no need to peel, just remove the stone. Canned peaches can be blended. When juicing, pears need their stalks removed but everything else, cores and seeds, can stay. Peel and core when blending. Use pears that are just short of fully ripe — you want the natural sweetness that comes with ripening but with a little crunch to make juicing easier. Pear (and apple) juice discolours quickly, so add citrus juice and drink immediately. Nashi pears can be treated like apples. The best plums are pleasantly scented, yield slightly when pressed and have a whitish bloom on the skin. Stone, then use in a juicer or blender. Prunes are dried plums — use them pitted.

49

Make this in the mellow months of autumn, when the orchards are heavy with sun-ripened fruit.

minted apple orchard

6 apples, stalks removed
3 pears, stalks removed
20 g (1 cup) mint leaves, plus extra to garnish

Juice the apples, pears and mint leaves through a juice extractor. Stir to combine and drink straight away. Garnish with a sprig of mint if desired. Makes 2 large glasses.

Don't just grapple with a cold, tackle it to the ground with this vitamin-C-rich apple and zucchini drink.

zapple

6 apples, stalks removed
2 zucchini (courgette)
3 cm (1¼ inch) piece ginger
ice cubes, to serve

Juice the apples, zucchini and ginger through a juice extractor. Stir to combine and serve over ice. Makes 2 large glasses.

minted apple orchard

Juice in bulk and fill your best bowl — your guests will be pleased as punch.

apricot fruit spritzer

500 ml (2 cups) apricot nectar
250 ml (1 cup) apple juice
250 ml (1 cup) orange juice
500 ml (2 cups) soda water
8 ice cubes

Put the apricot nectar, apple juice, orange juice, soda water and ice cubes into a large jug and stir to combine. Makes 4 medium glasses.

Everyone knows apricots look like cute little bottoms. They're also very good for you. Grab them while you can.

apricot, orange and ginger juice

10 apricots, stones removed
6 oranges, peeled
3 cm (1¼ inch) piece ginger
ice cubes, to serve

55

Juice the apricots, oranges and ginger through a juice extractor. Stir to combine and serve over ice. Makes 2 large glasses.

The sweetest member of the rose family, peaches bring a flush of unadulterated good health to the cheeks.

peach, kiwi and apple juice

4 peaches, stones removed
6 kiwifruit, peeled
3 apples, stalks removed

Juice the peaches, kiwifruit and apples through a juice extractor. Stir to combine. Makes 2 large glasses.

Like a southern belle with a headache, this is a smooth number with bite.

spiky peach

8 peaches, stones removed
1 small pineapple, peeled
10 g (1/2 cup) mint leaves
2 cm (3/4 inch) piece ginger

Juice the peaches, pineapple, mint and ginger through a juice extractor. Stir to combine. Makes 2 large glasses.

Thick and smooth, this drink gives the mind and body a gentle nudge into the new day.

peach and rockmelon juice

4 peaches
1/2 rockmelon (or other orange-fleshed melon), peeled,
  seeded and chopped
600 ml (21 fl oz) orange juice
12 ice cubes
1 tablespoon lime juice

Cut a small cross in the base of the peaches. Put them in a heatproof bowl and cover with boiling water. Leave for 1–2 minutes, then remove with a slotted spoon and plunge into cold water. Remove the skin and stones, and chop the flesh into bite-size pieces. Blend the peaches, rockmelon, orange juice and ice cubes in a blender until smooth. If the juice is too thick, add a little iced water. Stir through the lime juice. Makes 2 large glasses.

Add a little heat to sun-warmed peaches with a pinch of
freshly grated nutmeg.

fuzzy peach

6 peaches, stones removed
1 lemon, peeled
large pinch freshly grated nutmeg
250 ml (1 cup) dry ginger ale
ice cubes, to serve

Juice the peaches and lemon through a juice extractor. Stir through the
nutmeg and dry ginger ale. Serve over ice. Makes 2 large glasses.

Mint leaves plucked fresh from the plant is one of life's surest pick-me-ups.

pear and mint frappé

4 pears, peeled, cored and chopped
2 teaspoons roughly chopped mint
3 teaspoons caster (superfine) sugar
10 ice cubes
mint leaves, to garnish

Blend the pears, mint and sugar in a blender until smooth. Add the ice cubes and blend until smooth. Serve garnished with the extra mint leaves. Makes 2 medium glasses.

Peppermint is well known as a stomach calmer and its fresh aroma can also lift your mood.

pear, melon and peppermint juice

3 pears, stalks removed
1/2 small rockmelon (or other orange-fleshed melon), peeled,
  seeded and chopped
few peppermint leaves
ice cubes, to serve

Juice the pears, rockmelon and peppermint leaves through a juice extractor. Stir to combine and serve over ice. Makes 4 small glasses.

Note: The best way to select a ripe melon is to use your nose — if it has a strong sweet fragrance and thick raised netting you can almost guarantee it is ready to eat.

pear, melon and peppermint juice

If orange juice doesn't do it for you any more, give this a go.

plum, orange and vanilla

10 small plums, stones removed
6 oranges, peeled
1/2 teaspoon natural vanilla extract (essence)
ice cubes, to serve

Juice the plums and oranges through a juice extractor. Stir through the vanilla and serve over ice. Makes 2 large glasses.

Note: Use the ripest plums you can find.

Some days you need calming drinks. Other days you don't.

sweet and spicy plum

10 small plums, stones removed
3 cm (1¼ inch) piece ginger
200 g (7 oz) cherries, pitted
3 oranges, peeled
20 g (1 cup) mint leaves
1 teaspoon honey
ice cubes, to serve

Juice the plums, ginger, cherries, oranges and mint through a juice extractor. Stir through the honey, mixing well, and serve over ice. Makes 2 medium glasses.

sweet and spicy plum

tropical-à-go-go Heady perfumes, sticky flesh, vibrant colours and bizarre shapes are common occurrences among plant life in the world's torrid zones. For the poor witless juicer (meaning you and I), to meet

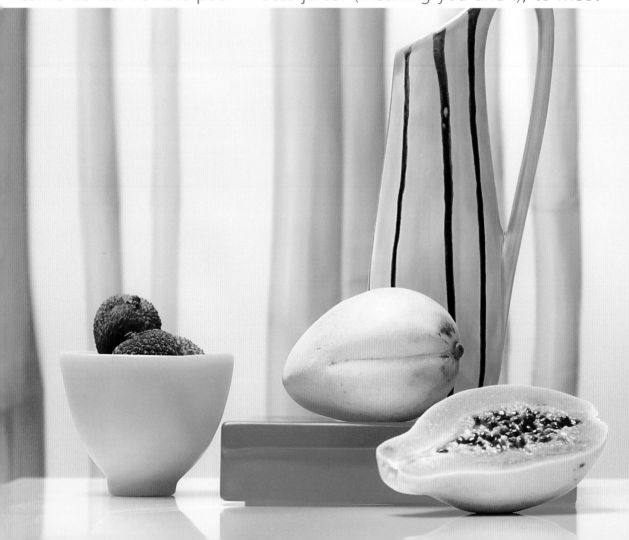

tropical fruit on their own terms is to enter into a strange world where one mango is never enough, loved ones turn combatants over the last passionfruit and pith helmuts seem entirely appropriate.

Blenders were probably designed with bananas in mind, even overripe ones. Just peel and chop, and mix with yoghurt, milk or ice cream. Fragrant, slightly acidic, pink or red-fleshed guavas have only a short season, so they mostly grace the juicing world already juiced. If you *are* using the fresh fruit, make sure it is fully ripe, then peel and dice. Small, green and furry, kiwi fruit are rich in vitamin C and potassium. Peel and dice for both juicer and blender. For lovers of mangoes, no effort is too great — cut the flesh over the bowl or blender to catch the drips. Choose fruit that is heavy, with a sweet, rich scent. Some juicers don't mind melon skin, be it honeydew or orange-fleshed melon such as rockmelon, but if in doubt cut the flesh away, deseed and chop. The riper the fruit, the sweeter the juice. Only when a papaya is fully ripe, should you seize the moment. Halve, remove the seeds and scoop out the flesh. Retain the seeds if you want; they are edible. To seed or not to seed passionfruit. To avoid any grittiness, strain the pulp before blending. Not to be confused with papaya, pawpaw is yellow-skinned, sweet and fragrant: ideal for the blender. A giant among juicing fruit, the pineapple makes an excellent base ingredient. Chop finely and remove the eyes if blending. Choose ones that feel heavy for their size and have a strong perfume. All parts of a watermelon are edible — remove the seeds if that takes your fancy, or look out for seedless varieties.

Get your motor running with this energy blast.

banana starter

2 bananas, chopped
100 g (3$\frac{1}{2}$ oz) frozen blueberries
1 red apple, cored
300 ml (10$\frac{1}{2}$ fl oz) apple juice
2 ice cubes

Blend the banana, frozen blueberries, apple, apple juice and ice cubes in a blender until smooth. Makes 4 small glasses.

Factor in 8 scoops of sorbet — one for the blender, one for me, one for the blender …

banana, kiwi and lemon frappé

2 bananas, chopped
3 kiwifruit, peeled and chopped
4 scoops lemon sorbet

Blend the banana, kiwifruit and sorbet in a blender until smooth. Makes 2 medium glasses.

banana, kiwi and lemon frappé

An excellent antioxidant, turn to this drink when you've been hitting the other grape juice a little too hard.

kiwi, grape and orange juice

6 kiwifruit, peeled
500 g (1 lb 2 oz) green seedless grapes
3 oranges, peeled
1 large passionfruit

Juice the kiwifruit, grapes and oranges through a juice extractor. Stir through the passionfruit pulp. Makes 2 large glasses.

The sweetest and gentlest of the melons, honeydew is the

perfect companion to tart and tangy lemon juice.

kiwi, honeydew and lemon juice

6 kiwifruit, peeled
1 honeydew melon, peeled, seeded and chopped
1 lemon, peeled

Juice the kiwifruit, honeydew and lemon through a juice extractor. Stir to combine. Makes 2 medium glasses.

Mango juice dribbling down hands and arms is part of the pleasure, but try and get it in the blender.

mango summer haze

2 mangoes, chopped
500 ml (2 cups) orange juice
55 g (1/4 cup) caster (superfine) sugar
500 ml (2 cups) sparkling mineral water
ice cubes, to serve
mango slices, to garnish, optional

Blend the mango, orange juice and sugar in a blender until smooth. Stir through the mineral water. Serve over ice and garnish with fresh mango slices, if desired. Makes 6 large glasses.

Mango has never had it so good — cosseted and surrounded by fizzy sweetness.

mango and mandarin chill

1 mango, sliced
500 ml (2 cups) mandarin juice
125 ml (1/2 cup) lime juice cordial
375 ml (1 1/2 cups) soda water
2 tablespoons caster (superfine) sugar
ice cubes, to serve

Freeze the mango for about 1 hour, or until semi-frozen. Combine the mandarin juice, cordial, soda water and sugar in a jug. Put the mango slices and some ice cubes into each glass, then pour in the juice mixture. Makes 2 medium glasses.

Note: For those with a sensitive sweet tooth, add the sugar to taste only at the end.

mango summer haze

Alive with intense flavours, this sweet syrup lifts fizzy water
into the realm of the divine.

passionfruit syrup

6 panama or large passionfruit
125 ml (1/2 cup) lemon juice
115 g (1/2 cup) caster (superfine) sugar

Combine the passionfruit pulp, lemon juice, sugar and 500 ml (2 cups)
water in a saucepan over high heat. Stir until the sugar has dissolved.
Bring to the boil, then reduce to a simmer and cook for 1 1/2 hours or until
reduced by half and slightly syrupy. Allow to cool, then strain, pressing on
the solids. Pour into a very clean glass jar or bottle and seal. Refrigerate
for up to 2 weeks. Makes 375 ml (1 1/2 cups).

Note: To serve, pour a little syrup into a glass with ice and top with soda
water, lemonade or dry ginger ale.

The wrinklier the passionfruit, the sweeter the pulp, so get down with an oldie.

passionfruit lime crush

6 panama or large passionfruit
185 ml (3/4 cup) lime juice cordial
750 ml (3 cups) dry ginger ale
crushed ice, to serve

Combine the passionfruit pulp, cordial and dry ginger ale in a large jug and mix together well. Half fill 4 large glasses with crushed ice and add the passionfruit mixture. Makes 4 large glasses.

passionfruit syrup

Bewitch yourself with this tingly little number.

fresh pineapple juice with mandarin sorbet

1 large pineapple, peeled
250 ml (1 cup) dry ginger ale
4 scoops mandarin sorbet

Juice the pineapple through a juice extractor. Combine the pineapple juice and dry ginger ale in a large jug and chill. Stir to combine, pour into 2 glasses and top each with 2 scoops of sorbet. Makes 2 medium glasses.

Sweet yet slightly astringent, this drink can catch you off your guard.

pineapple delight

1/2 pineapple, peeled and chopped
500 ml (2 cups) lemonade
2 tablespoons lime juice
mint leaves, to garnish

87

Blend the pineapple in a blender for 1–2 minutes, or until as smooth as possible. Pour the lemonade into a jug and stir through the pineapple purée. Add the lime juice and mix well. Serve garnished with mint leaves. Makes 4 small glasses.

fresh pineapple juice with mandarin sorbet

Think plump and juicy when choosing strawberries. Repeat out loud: plump and juicy.

watermelon and strawberry slushy

2 kg (10 cups) chopped watermelon (about 1 large watermelon)
250 g (9 oz) strawberries, hulled
2 teaspoons caster (superfine) sugar

Combine the watermelon, strawberries and sugar in a bowl. Save some watermelon for garnishing. Blend the mixture in batches in a blender until smooth, then pour into a shallow metal tray. Cover with plastic wrap and freeze for 2–3 hours, or until the mixture begins to freeze. Return to the blender and blend quickly to break up the ice. Pour into 6 glasses, then cut the reserved watermelon into 6 small triangles and fix one onto the edge of each glass. Makes 6 medium glasses.

Create a thousand-and-one Arabian Nights of your own with this petal-scented sparkler.

watermelon rosewater slushy

600 g (3 cups) chopped watermelon
1 teaspoon rosewater
1 teaspoon lemon juice
500 ml (2 cups) lemonade

Blend the watermelon in a blender until smooth. Combine with the rosewater, lemon juice and lemonade, then pour into a shallow metal tray. Cover with plastic wrap and freeze for 2 hours, or until just solid around the edges. Return to the blender and blend until thick and slushy. Makes 4 large glasses.

Note: Watermelons are now available almost all year, but tend to be sweeter in the warmer months. Choose one that feels heavy for its size.

watermelon and strawberry slushy

citrus burst Short, sharp, tart, tangy, testy, zesty, mouth-puckering, muscle-clenching, jaw-clinching, eye-popping, shackle-shaking, thirst-quenching, stomach-clutching, sobriety-inducing, temper-tampering, sour-pussing, grizzly-gripping, gusto-making, constitution-shaking, mood-meddling, spine-tingling, total body-cleansing, fleet-of-footing, exhilarating, illuminating and straight-talking citrus! Believe it or not.

The largest of the citrus, grapefruit also pack a punch. Choose heavy fruit with unblemished skins. Pink and ruby varieties are sweeter and result in prettily-coloured juices. Grapefruit can be used in a juicer, with or without the peel (you get more pectin and antioxidants if the peel is added), in the blender, or halved and squeezed on a citrus press. A word of caution: if taking medication, consult your doctor before drinking large doses. The indispensable lemon has a dual purpose in juices. First, for flavour, and second, as a means of preventing fruit such as apples and pears from discolouring. Thin-skinned organic lemons can be juiced without peeling. Otherwise, peel thinly, leaving as much of the white pith as possible, then juice. As with lemons, limes can be used to prevent discolouration of fruits. The flavour also cuts through the richness of other fruits, particularly tropical ones. Roll limes on the bench top to get the most juice out of them. Use on a citrus press or peel and add to a juicer. Buy oranges that feel heavy and have tight skin. Use on a citrus press, juice or blend. Navel oranges are nearly always seedless, so are a good choice. Blood oranges are sweeter and smaller than standard oranges and ensure a great colour in drinks — grab them when in season. Mandarins (and other small citrus such as clementines and tangerines) are smaller and often a bit sweeter than oranges. Juicy clementines have a slight hint of acidity. They go well with warming flavours such as cinnamon and cloves in infused drinks.

Drink this baby and you will soon be back in the pink.

think pink

3 pink grapefruit, peeled
250 g (9 oz) strawberries, hulled
375 ml (1 1/2 cups) guava juice
ice cubes, to serve

Juice the grapefruit and strawberries through a juice extractor. Stir through the guava juice and serve over ice. Makes 2 large glasses.

A frou frou fancy for a girly afternoon.

pink pom pom

4 pink grapefruit, peeled
500 g (1 lb 2 oz) black seedless grapes
3 large passionfruit
1 teaspoon pomegranate syrup
honey, to taste
ice cubes, to serve

Juice the grapefruit and grapes through a juice extractor. Stir through the passionfruit pulp, pomegranate syrup and honey and serve over ice. Makes 2 large glasses.

think pink

Beat granny at her own game with this zesty lemon refresher — just make sure you save her a glass.

just-like-grandma-made lemonade

15 lemons
330 g (1½ cups) sugar
ice cubes, to serve
lemon balm leaves, to serve
lemon slices, to serve

Juice the lemons in a citrus press. Put the lemon juice and any pulp in a large non-metallic bowl. Add the sugar and 125 ml (½ cup) boiling water and stir until the sugar has dissolved. Add 1.5 litres (6 cups) water and stir well. Transfer to a large jug, add ice cubes and float the lemon balm leaves and lemon slices on top. Makes 6 small glasses.

Running low on funds? Take a tip from childhood and set up a stall of your own.

homemade lemonade

685 ml (2¾ cups) lemon juice
275 g (1¼ cups) caster (superfine) sugar
ice cubes, to serve
mint leaves, to garnish

Combine the lemon juice and sugar in a large bowl and stir until the sugar has dissolved. Pour into a large jug. Add 1.25 litres (5 cups) water, stir well and chill. Serve over ice, garnished with a few mint leaves. Makes 6 medium glasses.

homemade lemonade

Burst onto the scene with this feel-good golden blast.

pine, lime and strawberry burst

1 pineapple, peeled
2 limes, peeled

500 g (1 lb 2 oz) strawberries, hulled

Juice the pineapple, limes and strawberries through a juice extractor. Stir to combine. Makes 2 medium glasses.

Take the sting out of an early start with this citrus antidote.

citrus sting

2 limes
3 grapefruit
6 oranges
honey, to taste

Juice the limes, grapefruit and oranges in a citrus press. Stir through the honey. Makes 4 large glasses.

An extravaganza of succulent stone fruit, tempered with the refreshing tang of oranges.

summer orange

3 oranges, peeled
5 small plums, stones removed
4 peaches, stones removed
10 apricots, stones removed

Juice the oranges, plums, peaches and apricots through a juice extractor.
Stir to combine. Makes 2 large glasses.

If only all of our crushes could be so sweet.

orange citrus crush

12 navel oranges
zest and juice of 1 lime
sugar, to taste
ice cubes, to serve

Segment 2 of the oranges and juice the remainder in a citrus press — don't strain the juice, you can keep the pulp in it. Add the lime zest and juice to the orange juice. Add the orange segments and sugar. Stir to combine and serve over ice. Makes 4 medium glasses.

Note: The juice of navel oranges will turn bitter within minutes of juicing, so drink this juice immediately. Use blood oranges when they're in season.

orange citrus crush

Too old for an ice cream spider? Go for this grown-up version.

orange sorbet soda

500 ml (2 cups) orange juice
250 ml (1 cup) lemonade
2–4 scoops lemon sorbet

Combine the orange juice and lemonade in a jug. Pour into 2 large glasses and top each with 1–2 scoops sorbet. Makes 2 large glasses.

All the colours of the fruity rainbow swirled together.

orange and mixed fruit frappé

10 dried apricot halves
200 g (7 oz) raspberries
1 banana, chopped
1 mango, chopped
500 ml (2 cups) orange juice
1 tablespoon mint leaves
6 ice cubes

Put the dried apricots in a heatproof bowl with 60 ml (1/4 cup) boiling water. Set aside for 10 minutes, or until plump, then drain and roughly chop. Blend the apricots, raspberries, banana, mango, orange juice, mint leaves and ice cubes in a blender until smooth. Makes 4 medium glasses.

the vegetable garden Just like getting sand between the toes, this chapter is all about getting soil between the teeth. No matter how much you scrub some of these fellas, you'll never convince them to shed their earthy goodness. As someone once said, you can take the carrot out of the garden but you can't take the garden out of the carrot. The uninitiated may like to start with small servings of these healthy elixirs.

Super rich in iron and beta-carotenes, **beetroot** is not for the mild-mannered juicer. Cut its earthy richness with citrus. To prepare, give beetroot a seriously good scrubbing and cut off any green stems. Cut the crown away, chop and add to the juicer. Sweet **carrots** make a great base juice and are limited only by the fact that they oxidize quickly. Use with citrus juice to help prevent this. Trim tops, then juice. Salty, watery **celery** needs rinsing under running water before juicing; add the leaves too, if you want. Buy celery with crisp, fresh stems. For sheer refreshing good value, try **cucumber.** Choose firm ones (the variety doesn't really matter) with no signs of bruising and store in the refrigerator, wrapped in plastic. No need to peel, just wash and juice. **fennel** is a funny one. Just when you think you've discovered every way that it can be prepared, along comes another, such as juicing. Use baby bulbs where possible, or larger, more mature ones for a headier flavour. **garlic** embodies the great and good from the garden. Peel the cloves before you juice. **green leafy vegetables** like spinach and watercress are excellent sources of antioxidants and phytochemicals. Use leaves straight from the refrigerator, while they are still a bit stiff, or juice with other ingredients. Rinse spinach well or soak in ice-cold water for 1–2 minutes to get rid of sand and grit. Leaves and **herbs** need to be bundled together or alternated with other, juicier ingredients. Juice on slow. Use good quality **tomatoes** to get the best flavour and nutritional value.

Add body and bounce to your natural vitality with this spicy little number.

vitalizing beetroot, carrot and ginger juice

1 beetroot, scrubbed
6 carrots
3 cm (1¼ inch) piece ginger, peeled

Juice the beetroot, carrots and ginger through a juice extractor. Stir to combine. Makes 2 small glasses.

Down a tumbler of this nourishing blend for a detox that matches style with substance.

dinner in a glass

1 beetroot, scrubbed
10–12 carrots
2 green apples, stalks removed
2 English spinach leaves
2 celery stalks

Juice the beetroot, carrots, apples, spinach and celery through a juice extractor. Stir to combine and serve chilled. Makes 2 large glasses.

vitalizing beetroot, carrot and ginger juice

Even the meanest machine needs the occasional tune-up.

green machine

6 celery stalks
2 apples, stalks removed
125 g (4 1/2 oz) alfalfa sprouts
10 g (1/2 cup) flat-leaf (Italian) parsley
10 g (1/2 cup) mint leaves

Juice the celery, apples, alfalfa, parsley and mint through a juice extractor.
Stir to combine. Makes 2 medium glasses.

Sticks and stones may break my bones but juice helps me forget all about it.

sticks and stones

6 celery stalks
5 small peaches, stones removed
1/2 lemon, peeled
7 g (1/4 cup) basil leaves
ice cubes, to serve

Juice the celery, peaches, lemon and basil through a juice extractor. Stir to combine and serve over ice. Makes 2 medium glasses.

green machine

Don't be a dill, revive and survive with this smart concoction.

cucumber, apple and dill juice

2 large cucumbers
9 apples, stalks removed
2 tablespoons dill
1 lemon, peeled
ice cubes, to serve

Juice the cucumbers, apples, dill and lemon through a juice extractor. Stir
to combine and serve over ice. Makes 2 medium glasses.

Enhance your cool factor with a chilled shot of cucumber.

cool as a cucumber

3 large cucumbers
3 limes, peeled
20 g (1 cup) mint leaves
1½ tablespoons caster (superfine) sugar

Juice the cucumbers, limes and mint through a juice extractor. Stir through the sugar. Makes 2 large glasses.

Your mum always told you to eat your greens, but better still, drink them!

green shot

30 g (1 1/2 cups) flat-leaf (Italian) parsley
1 medium cucumber
1/2 teaspoon caster (superfine) sugar
1/2 teaspoon lemon juice

Juice the parsley and cucumber through a juice extractor, saving a little cucumber for garnishing. Stir through the sugar until the sugar has fully dissolved. Chill well, then stir through the lemon juice and garnish with cucumber sticks. Serve immediately. Makes 6 shot glasses.

One, two, three … down the hatch.

herbal tonic

20 g (1 cup) flat-leaf (Italian) parsley
20 g (1 cup) mint leaves
15 g (1/2 cup) coriander (cilantro) leaves
3 cm (1 1/4 inch) piece ginger
500 ml (2 cups) tonic water
ice cubes, to serve

Juice the parsley, mint, coriander and ginger through a juice extractor then add 2 tablespoons water to help push the juice through. Stir through the tonic water and serve over ice. Makes 2 large glasses.

green shot

Life can be a marathon *and* a sprint, so when you need a fuel injection, reach for the juicer.

spinach energizer

50 g (2 cups) baby English spinach leaves
1 large cucumber
3 apples, stalks removed
3 celery stalks
1 baby fennel
10 g (1/2 cup) parsley

Juice the spinach, cucumber, apples, celery, fennel and parsley through a juice extractor. Stir to combine. Makes 2 large glasses.

Butterflies can flutter at any time. Soothe them away with this calming tonic.

tummy calmer

50 g (2 cups) English spinach leaves
400 g (14 oz) cabbage
4 apples, stalks removed

Juice the spinach, cabbage and apples through a juice extractor. Stir to combine. Makes 2 small glasses.

Knocks a virgin mary into touch — spicy, hot and red in tooth and claw.

gazpacho in a glass

6 vine-ripened tomatoes
1 red capsicum (pepper)
1 lemon, peeled
2 large cucumbers
10 g (1/2 cup) parsley
1 garlic clove
dash Tabasco sauce
ice cubes, to serve
extra virgin olive oil, to serve, optional

Juice the tomatoes, capsicum, lemon, cucumbers, parsley and garlic through a juice extractor. Stir through the Tabasco, to taste. Serve over ice with a drizzle of extra virgin olive oil, if desired. Makes 2 large glasses.

This drink is a seriously good tipple in its own right, but if you must add a slug of vodka, we promise not to tell.

virgin mary

750 ml (3 cups) tomato juice
1 tablespoon Worcestershire sauce
2 tablespoons lemon juice
1/4 teaspoon ground nutmeg
few drops Tabasco sauce
12 ice cubes
2 lemon slices, halved

Put the tomato juice, Worcestershire sauce, lemon juice, nutmeg and Tabasco sauce in a large jug and stir to combine. Blend the ice cubes in a blender for 30 seconds, or until the ice is crushed to 125 ml (1/2 cup). Pour the tomato juice mixture into 4 glasses and add the crushed ice and lemon slices. Season with salt and pepper. Makes 4 small glasses.

gazpacho in a glass

cinnamon, spice and all things nice The spice cupboard is a many splendoured thing: cloves and vanilla beans, cardamom pods, cinnamon sticks and aromatic nutmeg. Pound or grind, pulp and chop,

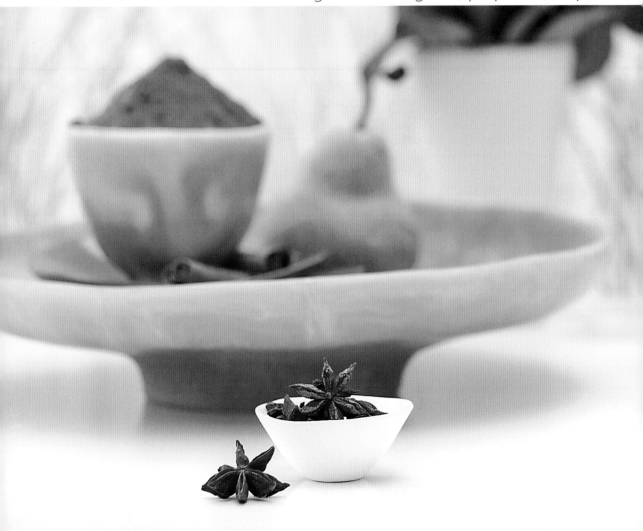

blend and infuse your way to soothing brews. Not every juice has to be all snap and crackle, you know. Look deep into your cupboard and discover ingredients full of depth and character, just waiting their turn.

Luxuriously aromatic, flower waters such as orange and rose are needed in small amounts only. Follow recipe suggestions. Fresh flowers such as lavender and edible rose petals are useful too: infuse and strain. Good old ginger. Knobbly, beige-coloured and a rhizome to boot, but still we can't get enough of it. With good reason, too: it calms an upset tummy, aids the digestion and gets a sluggish circulation into action. Generally, no need to peel or slice, just wash and use in the juicer. If it's fibrous, it may be easier to grate. Ground spices such as cardamom, cinnamon, cloves and cumin are great for adding warmth and depth to drinks. In their whole form, cardamom pods and cinnamon sticks can be used in infused drinks; freshly grated nutmeg brings a spicy warmth; and star anise adds a mild liquorice edge to drinks. For the best flavour, use the fresh spice if possible and grind it yourself as needed. A sticky, sweet-sour pulp, tamarind is sold in blocks that contain the plant's seeds or as ready-made concentrated paste in jars. To use, cut off a little, mix with hot water, then press through a sieve with a spoon to extract the pulp. Store in the refrigerator for up to a year. The humble tea bag isn't so humble after all. In infusions they go particularly well with citrus and fresh herbs. Good-quality vanilla pods have a warm, caramel vanilla aroma and flavour, and should be soft, not hard or dry. You can also use natural vanilla extract (essence) but beware of cheap copies. The pod can be reused: wash in cold water, then dry and store.

Use the best quality maple syrup you can find, then make this for your favourite mountie.

cinnamon, maple and pear frappé

400 g (14 oz) canned pears in natural juice
1/2 teaspoon ground cinnamon
11/2 tablespoons pure maple syrup
12 large ice cubes

Blend the pears and juice, maple syrup, cinnamon and ice cubes in a blender until smooth. Makes 2 large glasses.

Steeping the fruit and spices deepens the flavour of this golden infusion

cinnamon and apple tea infusion

1 cinnamon stick
4 golden delicious apples, roughly chopped
3–4 tablespoons soft brown sugar
ice cubes, to serve

Put the cinnamon stick, apple, brown sugar and 1 litre (4 cups) water into a pan. Bring to the boil, then reduce the heat and gently simmer for 10–15 minutes, or until the flavours have infused and the apple has softened. Remove from the heat and cool slightly, then chill. Strain and serve over lots of ice. Makes 2 medium glasses.

Play it again, Sam. Evoke the romance of Casablanca with this fragrant and exotic juice.

orange blossom citrus refresher

6 oranges, peeled
20 g (1 cup) mint leaves
1 1/2 teaspoons orange flower water
1 teaspoon pomegranate syrup
ice cubes, to serve
mint sprigs, to garnish
pomegranate syrup, extra, to serve, optional

Juice the oranges and mint leaves through a juice extractor. Stir through the orange flower water and pomegranate syrup and serve over ice, garnished with mint. Drizzle over a little more pomegranate syrup, if desired. Makes 2 medium glasses.

Create your own costume drama with this ladylike tonic.

lavender and rose lemonade

juice and zest of 2 lemons
15 g (1/2 oz) English lavender flowers, stripped from their stems
110 g (1 1/2 cups) sugar
1/2 teaspoon rosewater
edible pale pink rose petals, to garnish, optional

Put the lemon zest, lavender flowers, sugar and 500 ml (2 cups) boiling
water into a heatproof jug and mix well. Cover with plastic wrap and set
aside for 15 minutes. Strain, then stir through the lemon juice, rosewater
and enough cold water to make 1 litre (4 cups). Chill well. Stir to combine
and serve garnished with rose petals, if desired. Makes 6 small glasses.

Note: Add more water, if preferred, for a milder flavour.

lavender and rose lemonade

Strong and spicy, line up the shot glasses and find out who's really the tough guy.

red ginger

500 g (1 lb 2 oz) red seedless grapes
10 small plums, stones removed
2 limes, peeled
3 cm (1¼ inch) piece ginger
10 g (½ cup) mint leaves
ice cubes, to serve

Juice the grapes, plums, limes, ginger and mint through a juice extractor.
Stir to combine and serve over ice. Makes 4 shot glasses.

Just what you need to get yourself into gear when time is short and the to-do list is long.

pineapple ginger kick

1/2 pineapple, peeled
3 oranges, peeled
3.5 cm (1 1/2 inch) piece ginger
ice cubes, to serve

Juice the pineapple, oranges and ginger through a juice extractor. Stir to combine and serve over ice. Makes 2 small glasses.

red ginger

Instant winter warming with a zing of ginger and a healthy dose of vitamins.

warm ginger and carrot shots

2 kg (4 1b 8 oz) carrots
4 cm (1¹/₂ inch) piece ginger
1 tablespoon lemon juice
large pinch ground cinnamon
large pinch ground cumin
natural yoghurt, to serve, optional

Juice the carrots and ginger through a juice extractor. Transfer to a saucepan with the lemon juice, cinnamon and cumin. Stir over medium heat until just warmed through then pour into shot glasses or tall glasses. Top each glass with a small dollop of yoghurt and slightly swirl through. Makes 8 shot glasses or 2 large glasses.

Breathe deep and inhale the soothing aromas — a dreamy break is on its way.

ginger and lemon calm

3 cm (1¼ inch) piece ginger, sliced
1 lemon, thinly sliced
1 chamomile tea bag
honey, to taste

Put the ginger, lemon and tea bag in the bottom of a plunger or heatproof bowl and pour in 1 litre (4 cups) boiling water. Set aside to infuse for 10 minutes before plunging or straining. Serve with a little honey. Makes 4 small glasses.

warm ginger and carrot shots

This herbal hit will have you skipping all the way to work.

iced mint tea

4 peppermint tea bags
115 g (1/3 cup) honey
500 ml (2 cups) grapefruit juice
250 ml (1 cup) orange juice
mint sprigs, to garnish

Put the tea bags and 750 ml (3 cups) boiling water into a large heatproof jug. Set aside to infuse for 3 minutes. Discard the tea bags. Stir through the honey and set aside to cool. Stir through the grapefruit and orange juice, cover and chill. Stir to combine and serve garnished with mint sprigs. Makes 6 small glasses.

Develop a taste for island living with this piquant brew.

minty pineapple iced tea

1 pineapple or 500 ml (2 cups) pineapple juice
2 English breakfast tea bags
10 g (1/2 cup) mint leaves
ice cubes, to serve
mint sprigs, to garnish

Juice the pineapple through a juice extractor, then strain the juice. Put the tea bags, mint leaves and 1.25 litres (5 cups) boiling water into a large heatproof bowl. Set aside to infuse for 5 minutes. Discard the tea bags and mint. Stir through the pineapple juice and chill. Stir to combine and serve over ice, garnished with mint sprigs. Makes 4 medium glasses.

Mouth-puckeringly tart when straight, a dash of sugar makes tamarind lip-smackingly good.

tamarind cooler

2 teaspoons tamarind concentrate
3 tablespoons caster (superfine) sugar
20 g (1 cup) mint leaves
12 large ice cubes

Blend the tamarind, sugar, mint, ice cubes and 250 ml (1 cup) water in a blender until smooth. Makes 2 medium glasses.

A great winter blend, this will soon have you feeling warm and calm all over.

vanilla and apricot orange infusion

200 g (7 oz) dried apricots, chopped
1 vanilla bean, chopped
zest of 1 orange
55 g (¼ cup) caster (superfine) sugar
small pinch cloves, optional
ice cubes, to serve

Combine the apricots, vanilla bean, orange zest, sugar, cloves and 3 litres (12 cups) water in a large saucepan. Stir over high heat until the sugar has dissolved. Bring to the boil, then reduce the heat and gently simmer for 20 minutes. Set aside to cool. Strain and chill well. Stir to combine and serve over ice. Makes 6 medium glasses.

vanilla and apricot orange infusion

creamy concoctions Welcome to the world of the blender. A place of creamy, dreamy, silky, smoothy, cruisy, woozy, bluesy blends. We're talking no more Mr Second Fiddle, no more Mr Waiting in the Wings for the blender — dairy-based drinks are where it's at. Low-fat, no-fat, whole cream milk, even buttermilk: it loves them all. Fruit yoghurts, frozen yoghurts: perfect! Ice cream: delicious!

Weighing in at around 10 percent fat content, ice cream adds an unbeatable rich and creamy texture to smoothies. The better quality the ice cream, the better the resulting drink. Home-made ice creams made with raw eggs should be eaten within 3 days. Those without eggs will keep for longer but their flavour may change as they age. Be it skim, semi-skimmed or whole, milk is the bedrock upon which all other smoothies stand. Packed with calcium, protein and vitamins A and D (absent, however, from skimmed milks) it combines well with everything from macadamia nuts to figs. Lower fat milks result in a more watery drink. Buttermilk is made from pasteurized skim milk to which an acid-producing bacteria is added, thickening it and giving it a tangy taste. If using buttermilk in place of whole milk, omit any lemon or lime. Live yoghurt can support the digestive system by restoring natural gut bacteria. Of course, it also tastes good. Blend with well-established winners such as banana, mango and lime, but try also dried apricots, avocado and prunes. Don't worry overly if the low-fat wild berry yoghurt required by a recipe isn't available. Choose a similar one; the result will be just as good. Smoothies are ideal places for healthy additives to hide. Try sweet-tasting malted milk powder, made from dried and ground barley grains, or raw wheat germ, the extracted embryo of the wheat grain. Store wheat germ in the refrigerator, as it will go rancid due to its high oil content. Buy both from health food stores.

Best consumed on a Sunday with the papers by one hand and some waffles by the other.

blue maple

200 g (1 cup) low-fat blueberry fromage frais
185 ml (3/4 cup) low-fat milk
1 tablespoon maple syrup
1/2 teaspoon ground cinnamon
300 g (101/2 oz) frozen blueberries

Blend the fromage frais, milk, maple syrup, cinnamon and 250 g (9 oz) of the frozen blueberries in a blender until smooth. Serve topped with the remaining blueberries. Makes 2 medium glasses.

It's creamy, it's cold and it's berry, berry good.

berry slushy

300 g (10½ oz) frozen blueberries
150 g (5½ oz) raspberries
200 g (7 oz) vanilla yoghurt
250 ml (1 cup) milk
1 tablespoon wheat germ

Blend the frozen blueberries in a blender in short burts until starting to break up. Add the raspberries, yoghurt, milk and wheat germ and blend until smooth. Makes 2 large glasses.

blue maple

We could all do with one of these!

good start to the day

2 bananas, chopped
1 large mango, chopped
500 ml (2 cups) skim milk
500 ml (2 cups) orange juice or pink grapefruit juice

Blend the banana, mango, milk and orange or pink grapefruit juice in a blender until smooth. Pour into a jug and chill. Makes 4 small glasses.

The sort of drink to make us go weak at the knees.

caramelized banana shake

2 bananas, chopped
500 ml (2 cups) milk
2 scoops ice cream
1¹/2 tablespoons caramel sauce
1 tablespoon malted milk powder
pinch ground cinnamon

Blend the banana, milk, ice cream, caramel sauce, malted milk powder
and cinnamon in a blender until smooth. Makes 2 large glasses.

good start to the day

Serve in a parfait glass with long spoons and curly straws for the genuine diner experience.

passionfruit and vanilla ice cream whip

4 passionfruit
100 g (3¹/₂ oz) passionfruit yoghurt
500 ml (2 cups) milk
1 tablespoon caster (superfine) sugar
2–4 scoops vanilla ice cream

Push the passionfruit pulp through a sieve to remove the seeds. Transfer to a blender with the yoghurt, milk, sugar and 2 scoops of ice cream and blend until smooth. Pour into 2 glasses and top each with an extra scoop of ice cream, if desired. Makes 2 medium glasses.

Finish this off with a generous dribble of homemade passionfruit syrup — and let it finish you off.

passionfruit ice cream soda

6 passionfruit
2¹/₂ cups (625 ml) lemonade
2–4 scoops vanilla ice cream

Combine the passionfruit pulp (you will need 125 ml/¹/₂ cup) with the lemonade, pour into 2 glasses and top each with 1–2 scoops of ice cream. Serve with straws and long spoons. Makes 2 large glasses.

passionfruit ice cream soda

The avocado, master of disguise, is of course a fruit — and one that packs a protein punch.

avocado smoothie

1 small avocado, peeled, stone removed
500 ml (2 cups) milk
3 teaspoons honey
1/2 teaspoon natural vanilla extract (essence)

Blend the avocado, milk, honey and vanilla in a blender until smooth. Makes 2 medium glasses.

Don't judge a book by its cover, this Latin smoothie is a serious heartbreaker.

latin smoothie

1 small avocado, peeled, stone removed
125 ml (1/2 cup) condensed milk
juice of 1 lime
1 teaspoon natural vanilla extract (essence)
8 large ice cubes

Blend the avocado, condensed milk, lime juice, vanilla, ice cubes and 250 ml (1 cup) water in a blender until smooth. Makes 2 medium glasses.

avocado smoothie

Good prepared custard is readily available these days so feel free to take the easy road to sweetie heaven.

cinnamon and custard shake

375 ml (1 1/2 cups) milk
185 ml (3/4 cup) prepared custard
3 scoops vanilla ice cream
3 teaspoons honey
1 1/2 teaspoons ground cinnamon
ground cinnamon, extra, to serve

Blend the milk, custard, ice cream, honey and cinnamon until smooth and fluffy. Serve sprinkled with extra cinnamon. Makes 2 medium glasses.

A hot, creamy drink at bedtime is one of the few pleasures that lasts a lifetime.

creamy almond and vanilla shake

1 vanilla bean, halved lengthways
500 ml (2 cups) milk
80 g (1/2 cup) raw almonds, toasted
1 tablespoon pure maple syrup
1 teaspoon almond extract (essence)

Put the vanilla bean and milk into a saucepan and heat until almost boiling. Remove from the heat and set aside to infuse for 5 minutes. Return the pan to the heat and heat again until almost boiling. Remove the vanilla bean. Blend the milk, almonds, maple syrup and almond extract in a blender until thick and smooth. Makes 2 medium glasses.

Note: You can rinse the vanilla bean, let it dry and put it in an airtight container of caster (superfine) sugar. Use this vanilla sugar to flavour the drink in place of the maple syrup.

other ways to be a smoothie Take the road less travelled, the path little beaten, the track grown over with infrequent use. No longer do you need to look longingly at the dairy blends and think, if only

I could — you can! For among coconut and almond milk, tofu and soy milk you have friends stout of heart and firm of flavour. Know truly that dairy milk and its ilk don't necessarily rule the smoothie waves.

A lactose-free option, **almond milk** is not much thicker than milk, but its flavour is highly distinctive — similar to that of marzipan. It goes well with fruit such as dates, grapes, peaches and strawberries, and is available from health food stores and Italian delicatessens. Do not buy almond milk syrup, as it is very different. Fresh **coconut milk** from whole coconuts sounds impressive but, let's be honest, the canned variety is a tad easier to get at. Coconut cream produces drinks with a better consistency than coconut milk does, but is higher in fat. With both, buy good-quality brands to ensure milk with a lovely white colour. Light coconut milk can also be used; it has a thinner consistency. Blend with tropical fruit, raspberries and cherries. **silken tofu** may seem a strange inclusion here, but its textural qualities and nutritional benefits make it a welcome one. Its smoothie partners are tropical fruits such as banana and mango. Unlike cow's or goat's milk, **soy milk** does not contain lactose sugar or cholesterol. It has antioxidant benefits, but little calcium, so buy calcium-fortified soy milk if you're using it in place of dairy products. Soy milk can be quite sweet, so taste before adding other sweeteners such as honey. Use with warm flavours such as pears, cinnamon, dates and apricots. Soy yoghurt and soy ice cream are also good choices. **extras:** carob powder is sweet and has a similar flavour to chocolate, but without the fat. Lecithin meal is a natural soy-derived nutritional supplement, and its reputed properties range from aiding the liver to improving memory. Buy both from health food stores.

A veritable bazaar of flavours — sweet, nutty and smooth as a bolt of silk.

whipped nougat

200 g (1 cup) canned apricots in natural juice
500 ml (2 cups) almond milk
1½ teaspoons natural vanilla extract (essence)
1 teaspoon honey
few drops rosewater, optional
8 large ice cubes

Blend the undrained apricots, almond milk, vanilla, honey, rosewater and ice cubes in a blender until smooth. Makes 2 large glasses.

Cherries seem so indulgent — this drink will do nothing to change that impression.

almond cherry smoothie

375 ml (1½ cups) almond milk
400 g (14 oz) cherries, pitted
¼ teaspoon natural vanilla extract (essence)
pinch ground cinnamon
4 large ice cubes

Blend the almond milk, cherries, vanilla, cinnamon and ice cubes in a blender until smooth. Makes 2 large glasses.

Note: If you like a strong almond or marzipan flavour, add a dash of almond extract (essence).

almond cherry smoothie

When the island breeze is calling but work has you stalling,

take an instant holiday with this tropical shake.

coconut and mango shake

400 g (14 oz) fresh mango pulp
125 ml (1/2 cup) lime juice
125 ml (1/2 cup) coconut milk
2 teaspoons honey
3 teaspoons finely chopped mint
12 large ice cubes

Blend the mango pulp, lime juice, coconut milk, honey, mint and ice cubes
in a blender until thick and smooth. Chill well. Stir to combine. Makes
2 medium glasses.

Go the whole hog and serve this in cocktail glasses with lychees on toothpicks. And perhaps a splash of white rum.

pineapple and lychee creamy colada

1/3 pineapple, peeled and chopped
750 ml (3 cups) pineapple juice
500 g (1 lb 2 oz) canned lychees
2 tablespoons spearmint leaves
125 ml (1/2 cup) coconut cream
crushed ice

Blend the pineapple, pineapple juice, lychees and their juice and spearmint in a blender until smooth. Add the coconut cream and crushed ice and blend until thick and smooth. Makes 6 medium glasses.

pineapple and lychee creamy colada

Ascend to berry yoghurt heaven with a clear conscience.

strawberry lassi

250 g (9 oz) strawberries, hulled
300 g (10^1/$_2$ oz) strawberry soy yoghurt
2 tablespoons honey
4 ice cubes

Blend the strawberries, yoghurt, honey, ice cubes and 2^1/$_2$ tablespoons
water in a blender until smooth. Garnish with any leftover strawberries.
Makes 2 small glasses.

This drink is musky and full of promise, with gentle warmth.

spiced melon shake

1/4 teaspoon cardamom seeds
350 ml (12 fl oz) creamy soy milk
1/2 rockmelon (or other orange-fleshed melon), peeled, seeded
  and chopped
1 tablespoon honey
2 tablespoons ground almonds
4 ice cubes

Lightly crush the cardamom seeds in a mortar and pestle or with the back of a knife. Blend the cardamom and soy milk in a blender for 30 seconds. Strain the soy milk and rinse any remaining seeds from the blender. Return the strained milk to the blender, add the rockmelon, honey, almonds and ice cubes and blend until smooth. Makes 2 medium glasses.

strawberry lassi

Don't throw away black, spotted bananas, their lush ripeness is the highlight of this smoothie.

carob peanut smoothie

400 ml (14 oz) carob- or chocolate-flavoured soy milk
2 very ripe bananas, chopped
150 g (5¹/2 oz) silken tofu
2 tablespoons honey
1 tablespoon peanut butter

Blend the soy milk, banana, tofu, honey and peanut butter in a blender until smooth. Makes 2 medium or 4 small glasses.

Strong, sweet and powerful — a real super hero!

peanut choc power smoothie

500 ml (2 cups) chocolate-flavoured soy milk
125 g (4¹/₂ oz) silken tofu
60 g (¹/₄ cup) peanut butter
2 bananas, chopped
2 tablespoons chocolate sauce
8 large ice cubes

Blend the soy milk, tofu, peanut butter, banana, chocolate syrup and ice cubes in a blender until smooth. Makes 4 small glasses.

index

203

205

207

Published in 2011 by Murdoch Books Pty Limited

Murdoch Books Australia
Pier 8/9, 23 Hickson Road
Millers Point NSW 2000
Phone: +61 (0)2 8220 2000
Fax: +61 (0)2 8220 2558
www.murdochbooks.com.au

Murdoch Books UK Limited
Erico House, 6th Floor
93–99 Upper Richmond Road
Putney, London SW15 2TG
Phone: +44 (0)20 8785 5995
Fax: +44 (0)20 8785 5985
www.murdochbooks.co.uk

Chief Executive: Juliet Rogers
Publishing Director: Chris Rennie

Publisher: Lynn Lewis
Senior Designer: Heather Menzies
Design Layout: Handpress Graphics
Editorial Coordinator: Liz Malcolm
Production: Joan Beal

208

National Library of Australia Cataloguing-in-Publication Data
Title: Juices and Smoothies. ISBN: 978-1-74196-948-1(pbk.)
Series: New chubbie. Notes: Includes index. Subjects: Fruit juices. Vegetable juices. Smoothies (Beverages).
Dewey Number: 641.875

Printed by 1010 Printing International.
PRINTED IN CHINA

IMPORTANT: Those who might be at risk from the effects of salmonella poisoning (the elderly, pregnant women,
young children and those suffering from immune deficiency diseases) should consult their doctor with any
concerns about eating raw eggs.

OVEN GUIDE: You may find cooking times vary depending on the oven you are using. For fan-forced ovens,
as a general rule, set the oven temperature to 20°C (35°F) lower than indicated in the recipe.